FAMILY Life ISSUES

Life in the
Sandwich Generation

By Kay Meyer

CPH ™
SAINT LOUIS

Editor: Thomas J. Doyle
Series Editor: Rodney L. Rathmann
Editorial assistant: Phoebe W. Wellman

Write to Library for the Blind, 1333 S. Kirkwood Road, St. Louis, MO 63122-7295 to obtain *Life in the Sandwich Generation* in braille or large print for the visually impaired. Allow six months for processing.

Contents

Introduction

▲ How to Use This Course

This course has been especially prepared for use in small group settings. It may, however, also be used as a self-study or in a traditional Sunday morning Bible class.

▲ Planning for a Small Group Study

1. *Select a leader* for the course or a leader for the day. It will be the leader's responsibility to secure needed materials, to keep the discussion moving, and to help involve everyone.

2. *Emphasize sharing.* Your class will work best if the participants feel comfortable with one another and if all feel that their contributions to the class discussion are important and useful. Take the necessary time at the beginning of the course to get to know one another. You might share names, occupations, hobbies, etc. Share what you expect to gain from this course.

Invite participants to bring photos of their families to the first session to pass around as they introduce themselves and tell about the individual members of their families. Be open and accepting. Don't force anyone to speak. The course will be most helpful if participants willingly share deep feelings, problems, doubts, fears, and joys. That will require building an atmosphere of openness, trust, and caring between one another. Take time to build relationships among participants. That time will not be wasted.

3. Help participants apply the concepts included in each session. After each week's study, there is a list of suggested activities. An old Chinese proverb summarizes the "why?" of doing these activities during the week:

I hear and I forget;
I see and I remember;
I do and I understand.

These activities are included to help participants do and thus understand. Encourage everyone to take time to do them.

4. Encourage participants to invite their friends—including their unchurched friends—to be a part of this study.

▲ As You Plan to Lead the Group

1. Read this guide in its entirety before you lead the first session.

2. Use the Leaders Notes found in the back of this guide.

3. Pray each day for those who join the group.

4. As you prepare for each session, study the Bible texts thoroughly. Work through the exercises for yourself. Depend on the Holy Spirit. Expect His presence; He will guide you and cause you to grow. God will not let His Word return empty (Isaiah 55:11) as you study it both individually and with the others in the group.

5. But do not expect the Spirit to do your work for you. Start early. Prepare well. As time permits, do additional reading about the topic.

6. Begin and end with prayer.

7. Begin and end on time. Punctuality is a courtesy to everyone and can be a factor that will encourage discussion.

8. Find ways to keep the session informal. Meet in casual surroundings. Arrange seating so participants can face one another. Ask volunteers to provide refreshments.

9. Keep the class moving. Limit your discussion to questions of interest to the participants. Be selective. You don't need to cover every question and every Bible verse.

10. Build one another up through your fellowship and study. You have your needs; other group members have theirs. Together you have a lot to gain.

11. Be sensitive to any participants who may have needs related to the specific problems discussed in this course, especially anyone who may need Christian counseling and professional help.

12. Be a "gatekeeper." That means you may need to shut

the gate on one person while you open it for someone else. Involve everyone, especially those who hesitate to speak.

▲ If You Are Using This Study on Your Own

1. Each time you sit down to study a session, ask the Holy Spirit for guidance and counsel. Expect Him to work through His Word to encourage, motivate, and empower you to grow in your faith.

2. Study the Bible texts printed in the course with special care. God works through His Word. In it you will find power. Read each text slowly, several times.

3. Write answers in the spaces provided. Avoid the temptation to just "think" your responses. Writing will force you to be specific. It's in that specificity you are most likely to identify crucial issues for yourself. Check the Leaders Notes in the back of this guide for information you may find helpful as you go along.

4. Pray as you work. Ask God to show you what He wants you to see about Him, about yourself, and about your family situation.

The Big Squeeze 1

Ice Breaker

Share with a partner, whom you don't know well, an object from your purse or wallet that
1. makes you laugh or gives you great joy;
2. makes you angry, anxious, or afraid;
3. helps you to share your faith in Christ Jesus; and/or
4. reveals something unique about you.

Opening Prayer

O most gracious and heavenly Father, we give You thanks for our families. At times, Lord, we become squeezed with family responsibilities—caring for aging parents, nurturing our own children, and tending to everyone's needs—so that it seems we no longer have time or energy to care for our own needs. Enable us to find time to seek rescue and refuge in the promises You provide to us in Your Word. Thank You for sending Jesus into this world to rescue us from sin, death, and the power of Satan. Thank You for inviting us to bring the burdens of our responsibilities to Jesus and to find rest in Him. As we begin our study today, give us wisdom through Your Word so we may serve You and others with renewed joy. Provide us with Your Spirit's strength as we face our daily responsibilities as members of the sandwich generation. Amen.

Meet the Doe Family

My name is Jane. My mom moved in with my family "on a temporary basis" a year ago. We had no choice. Mom doesn't have enough money to move into a facility where she can receive the on-going care she needs. Her stroke left her unable to take care of herself. Although John and I both work, we can't afford the cost of full-time nursing care. Just the cost of the day nurse we hired to take care of mom while we work has stretched our budget to the breaking point. Since I'm an only child, I have the sole responsibility for caring for my mother.

The lives of our three children, Sara age 5; David, age 8; and Jonathan, age 15, changed when their grandma moved in. Our house is so small that Sara ended up sharing her room with Grandma. Although Sara loves her Grandma, Sara has had to adjust to Grandma's long naps and loud snoring.

The other day, David's teacher called to tell me that David cried because he hadn't been able to finish his homework. Unfortunately the night before, I got home late from work, John had a meeting at church, Jonathan had the stomach flu, Sara had a appointment to get her hair cut, and Mom cried and cried because she felt she was a burden to us. I wasn't able to help David with his homework.

Sound unrealistic? Millions of people today find themselves facing situations similar to the Doe family. How do you think Jane feels? What thoughts might Jane have as she assumes enormous responsibilities for her mother, husband, children, and work? Check all that might describe Jane's feelings. What other thoughts and feelings might Jane have?

_____ 1. My children are blessed having the opportunity to live with their grandma.

_____ 2. I must shoulder all of the responsibilities myself.

_____ 3. It will all get done.

_____ 4. No one understands the strain I'm under.

_____ 5. I hope my children will someday show me the kind of care I'm giving to my mom.

_____ 6. I sometimes feel angry toward those for whom I must care.

_____ 7. I feel used.

_____ 8. I'd love to run from the many responsibilities I have.

_____ 9. I don't have time for me.

_____10. I feel guilty for not having more to give.

_____11. God is unfair to expect me to cope with all this.

_____12. Something has to give or I will explode.

_____other _____

_____other _____

Now, go back and draw a star next to those thoughts or feelings you have had as you experienced the big squeeze of life in the sandwich generation—squeezed between responsibilities for aging parents and responsibilities for children.

Take time to share your story with a partner. Consider using the list of thoughts and feelings as a starting point to describe your life.

Squeezed, but Not Squashed

Read 1 Timothy 5:8 below.

▼▼▼▼▼▼▼▼▼▼▼▼▼▼▼▼▼▼▼▼▼▼▼▼▼

If anyone does not provide for his relatives, and especially for his immediate family, he has denied the faith and is worse than an unbeliever. (1 Timothy 5:8)

▲▲▲▲▲▲▲▲▲▲▲▲▲▲▲▲▲▲▲▲▲▲▲▲▲

1. How do you suppose Jane would respond to God's expectation expressed in this Bible verse? What thoughts or feelings come to mind as you think about this verse?

2. Consider your life—attitudes and actions. How well do you measure up to God's expectation? Check one.

_____Wonderfully

_____Okay

_____Miserably, at times

_____Could we discuss something else?

3. Because of sin, we all fail to live up to God's expectation, "Be perfect" (Matthew 5:48). When we are squeezed by the expectations of our parents and our children, we may fail to provide willingly and joyfully as God desires. God's Word reminds us of the refuge and rescue He waits to provide us when we experience the big squeeze. As you read Psalm 91, underline words and/or phrases that give you a clue that the author was experiencing some type of big squeeze.

▼▼▼▼▼▼▼▼▼▼▼▼▼▼▼▼▼▼▼▼▼▼▼▼▼▼

He who dwells in the shelter of the Most High
    will rest in the shadow of the Almighty.
I will say of the LORD, "He is my refuge and my fortress,
    my God, in whom I trust."
Surely He will save you from the fowler's snare
    and from the deadly pestilence.
He will cover you with His feathers,
    and under His wings you will find refuge;
    His faithfulness will be your shield and rampart.
You will not fear the terror of night,
    nor the arrow that flies by day,
nor the pestilence that stalks in the darkness,
    nor the plague that destroys at midday.
A thousand may fall at your side,
    ten thousand at your right hand,
    but it will not come near you.
You will only observe with your eyes
    and see the punishment of the wicked.
If you make the Most High your dwelling—
    even the LORD, who is my refuge—
then no harm will befall you,
    no disaster will come near your tent.
For He will command His angels concerning you
    to guard you in all your ways;
they will lift you up in their hands,
    so that you will not strike your foot against a stone.
You will tread upon the lion and the cobra;
    you will trample the great lion and the serpent.
"Because he loves Me," says the LORD,
        "I will rescue him;
    I will protect him, for he acknowledges
        My name.
    He will call upon Me, and I will answer him;
    I will be with him in trouble,
    I will deliver him and honor him.
With long life will I satisfy him
    and show him My salvation." (Psalm 91)

▲▲▲▲▲▲▲▲▲▲▲▲▲▲▲▲▲▲▲▲▲▲▲▲▲

4. Now, go back through the psalm with pen in hand and circle those phrases that indicate that although the author is experiencing a big squeeze, he has confidence that it will not squash him.

5. Draw a cross next to the words and/or phrases telling that God provides a refuge for those who experience the big squeeze in their lives.

6. Discuss with a partner how the images for refuge described in the psalm impact you as you consider life as the sandwich generation.

7. In spite of all of the personal trials, tribulations, and frustrations that St. Paul experienced in his lifetime, he had peace. Paul summarized the reason for his confidence and hope even as he faced conflict in Galatians 1:3–5.

Acknowledge God's love for you now by substituting your name for the pronouns in Galatians 1:3–5. Then have a partner read aloud the verses that include your name.

▼▼▼▼▼▼▼▼▼▼▼▼▼▼▼▼▼▼▼▼▼▼▼▼▼▼

Grace and peace to you (_____) from God our Father and the Lord Jesus Christ, who gave Himself for our sins to rescue us from the present evil age, according to the will of our God and Father, to whom be glory for ever and ever. Amen. (Galatians 1:3–5)

▲▲▲▲▲▲▲▲▲▲▲▲▲▲▲▲▲▲▲▲▲▲▲▲▲▲

8. God not only provides us refuge from the troubles of this world, He also has rescued us. From what has God rescued us?

9. How does knowing that God loves us so much that He willingly sent His only Son to suffer and die for us, enable us to face a big squeeze with comfort and encouragement?

Peace in the Midst of the Big Squeeze

God promises that as our faith is strengthened by the power of the Holy Spirit, He gives us peace. In His Word, Jesus invites us to come to Him when we are burdened and He will help us. In the passage that follows, underline Jesus' promises to those who come to Him in faith.

▼▼▼▼▼▼▼▼▼▼▼▼▼▼▼▼▼▼▼▼▼▼▼▼▼▼▼▼

Come to Me, all you who are weary and burdened, and I will give you rest. Take My yoke upon you and learn from Me, for I am gentle and humble in heart, and you will find rest for your souls. For My yoke is easy and My burden is light. (Matthew 11:28–30)

▲▲▲▲▲▲▲▲▲▲▲▲▲▲▲▲▲▲▲▲▲▲▲▲▲▲▲▲

Write a prayer thanking Him for His promises of rescue and refuge. Ask that as the Holy Spirit works through the study of God's Word, you might find renewed strength enabling you to serve God, yourself, and those for whom you are responsible—older relatives (parents, grandparents, etc.) and younger relatives (children, grandchildren, etc.).

Before the Next Session

1. Identify some of the challenges of caring for aging parents and/or relatives.

2. Identify some of the blessings of caring for aging parents and/or relatives.

3. Review daily the Bible passages studied in this session.

4. Record some new thoughts or feelings you might have concerning your life as the sandwich generation.

Closing Prayer

Pray the prayer you wrote earlier in this session.

Caring for Aging Parents

2

Ice Breaker

Choose one of the following sentence starters to talk about with a partner.

1. What I remember best about my grand-father/grandmother is ...

2. My earliest memory of my dad/mom was when he/she ...

3. My favorite family holiday tradition is ...

4. My first experience with the death of a loved one was ...

Opening Prayer

Dear God, You parent us with such love and patience. We praise You for the forgiveness, new life, and salvation that are ours through Jesus. Thank You for the privilege we have in Him of being able to call You our Father. Help us to show our love for You by the love, care, and concern we show for the earthly parents You have given us. As Your Holy Spirit works in our lives, make our faith strong. We pray in Jesus' name. Amen.

A Visit to the Doe Household

Remember me? I am Jane Doe. I told you a little bit about my family in the last session.

The decision to invite Mom to move in a year ago

was difficult. John and I discussed the options. The only one that seemed reasonable to me was to take Mom into our home. I mean she cared for me for 18 years. The least I can do is care for her during her last years. John did not agree with me. He listed reason after reason for not inviting Mom to live with us; too expensive, too busy, too much time, not enough room. ... I couldn't hear those reasons. Everytime I would begin to go along with John, intense guilt consumed me. Mom is my responsibility. I couldn't let her live her last years with strangers. How would I want my children to treat me during the last years of my life?

So Mom moved in amidst concerns by John. Life has been difficult during the past year. But we have also been blessed! We don't have enough money or time. Often we are too busy to spend time with the children. But God has provided us something of great value through Mom. I have the satisfaction of giving back to Mom a small portion of the love she never stopped giving to me. The kids have enjoyed getting to know Grandma more intimately. And the kids have discovered a joy in serving her. John continues to wrestle with the issues of space, time, money, etc., but has conceded recently that he wouldn't change anything. God has provided us strength to endure the challenges we have faced and peace in knowing that He is always with us.

1. Share some of the challenges you and/or your family have faced in caring for an aging parent.

2. Share some of the joys you and/or your family have experienced while caring for an aging parent.

The Sandwich Generation Speaks

Select the answer to each of the following questions that best reflects your attitude.

1. Which of the following discussions have you had with your parents regarding the time when they become older and possibly begin needing help?

_____Have not yet brought up the topic with them.

_____Have talked generally but made no plans.

_____Have discussed plans for finances, housing, and medical care but have not initiated any legal arrangements.

_____Have actually worked together to draw up legal documents for finances, housing, and medical care.

_____Don't know.

2. Which of the following situations do you fear *most* when you think about your parents getting older?

_____They'll suffer disabilities that will force them to live in a nursing home.

_____They'll die suddenly without the chance to say good-bye.

_____They'll end up in a hospital being kept alive by machines.

_____Their need for ongoing medical care will force them to sell their home or spend their life's savings.

_____Don't know.

3. Do you think it's an adult child's responsibility to care for his or her parents as they grow older?

_____Yes

_____No

_____Don't know.

4. Do you feel it is the child's responsibility to care for his or her parents even if they—parent(s) and child—have never gotten along well?

_____Yes

_____No

_____Don't know.

5. Would you favor or oppose your parents using up their savings to provide for their own long-term care, even if it meant that you would get no inheritance?

_____Favor

_____Oppose

_____Don't know.

6. Some adult children have helped their parents legally shelter their savings and property so that Mom or Dad can qualify for Medicaid nursing-home benefits. Would you consider doing this for your parents?

_____Yes

_____No

_____Don't know.

7. Would you consider placing your parents in a nursing home if they were too sick to care for themselves?

_____Yes

_____No

_____Don't know.

8. Would you consider asking your parents to move in with you if they could no longer live alone?

_____Yes

_____No

_____Don't know.

9. Suppose your parent was severely ill and unconscious in a hospital, having left written instructions that he or she not be kept alive by machines or major surgery. Would you

_____Insist doctors abide by your parent's instructions under all circumstances?

_____Overrule those instructions and authorize treatment if doctors recommend it?

_____Don't know.

These questions were asked in a recent Gallup poll. The answers provide a striking look at the hopes and fears of adult Americans who have living and aging parents. Hidden behind the averages provided in the Leaders Notes, are some surprises, especially when you look at how various age groups responded to the questions. While the poll results mirror the views of the baby boom generations (the sandwich generation), younger and older Americans have different things to say. Those age 18–29 may have had fewer heart-to-heart talks with their parents about growing old, but they're even more eager than the thirty- or forty-somethings to help. Perhaps a sense of realism comes with age. Those over 50 are more ready to say that nursing-home care might be an acceptable alternative.

1. Are there any surprises you found in the response percentages? If so, what?

2. How do your responses to each of the questions compare with the majority of Americans?

▼

3. Summarize the results of the Gallup Poll in two or three sentences.

4. How do the majority of Americans measure up to God's Word, "If anyone does not provide for his relatives, and especially for his immediate family, he has denied the faith and is worse than an unbeliever" (1 Timothy 5:8)?

5. How do you measure up?

God's Word Speaks

We seek the wisdom that only God can provide us in His Word as we wrestle with the issues that surround caring for aging parents.

First, what does God say about the elderly and our attitude and responsibility to them? Read the following passages with pen in hand. Underline significant words and/or phrases.

Rise in the presence of the aged, show respect for the elderly and revere your God. I am the LORD. (Leviticus 19:32)

Gray hair is a crown of splendor; it is attained by a righteous life. (Proverbs 16:31)

The glory of young men is their strength, gray hair the splendor of the old. (Proverbs 20:29)

Honor your father and your mother, so that you may live long in the land the LORD your God is giving you.(Exodus 20:12).

Children, obey your parents in the Lord, for this is right. "Honor your father and mother"—which is the first commandment with a promise—"that it may go well with you and that you may enjoy long life on the earth." (Ephesians 6:1–3)

▲▲▲▲▲▲▲▲▲▲▲▲▲▲▲▲▲▲▲▲▲▲▲▲▲▲▲▲▲

1. Summarize what God says our attitude and responsibility ought to be toward our aging parents.

2. How do you measure up to God's expectations for your attitude and responsibility toward your aging parents? Put a mark on the continuum to describe how well you live up to God's expectations. Explain your answer.

├───┤
success   failure

3. If honest, most of us would have to admit that we don't *always* live up to God's expectations. Often we may fail miserably. At times of failure we can confess the words of David the psalmist,

▼▼▼▼▼▼▼▼▼▼▼▼▼▼▼▼▼▼▼▼▼▼▼▼▼▼▼▼▼

¹Blessed is he
    whose transgressions are forgiven,
    whose sins are covered.
²Blessed is the man
    whose sin the LORD does not count against him
    and in whose spirit is no deceit.
³When I kept silent,
    my bones wasted away
    through my groaning all day long.
⁴For day and night
    Your hand was heavy upon me;
my strength was sapped
    as in the heat of summer.
⁵Then I acknowledged my sin to You
    and did not cover up my iniquity.
I said, "I will confess
    my transgression to the LORD"—
and You forgave
    the guilt of my sin.

• • • • • • • • • • • • • • • • • •

⁸I will instruct you and teach you
      in the way you should go;
    I will counsel you and watch over you.
⁹Do not be like the horse or the mule,
    which have no understanding
but must be controlled by bit and bridle
    or they will not come to you.
¹⁰Many are the woes of the wicked,
    but the LORD's unfailing love
    surrounds the man who trusts in Him.
¹¹Rejoice in the LORD and be glad, you righteous;
    sing, all you who are upright in heart!
    (Psalm 32:1–5, 8–11)

▲▲▲▲▲▲▲▲▲▲▲▲▲▲▲▲▲▲▲▲▲▲▲▲▲▲▲▲

4. What does God offer to all who have failed to live up to His high, "Be perfect" (Matthew 5:48), standards?

5. What comfort does God's Word provide to you for the times when you become angry, bitter, and/or overwhelmed by the responsibilities of caring for aging parents?

6. Reread verse 8. God provides His forgiven people with the assurance of His promises of hope and encouragement. Through His Word He strengthens us for our role of caregiver for aging parents. What opportunities *will you* have during the next week for God to "instruct you and teach you in the way you should go"?

7. Write a prayer of praise to God for the forgiveness He provides to you through faith in Christ Jesus

for the times you fail to live up to the expectations He has for you as you care for aging parents. Include a request for the Spirit's guidance, peace, and joy as you fulfill your responsibilities.

Before the Next Session

1. Identify some of the challenges of caring for children.

2. Identify some of the blessings of caring for children.

3. Review daily the Bible passages studied in this session and session 1.

4. Record some new thoughts or feelings you might have concerning your life as the sandwich generation.

Closing Prayer

Pray the prayer of praise you wrote earlier.

▼

Bringing Up Children

Ice Breaker

Share the answer to one of the following questions with a partner.

1. What are some of the most memorable times you spent with your children? What made them so memorable?

2. How might your child(ren) describe you?

3. If you could change one thing about your parenting, what would it be?

4. Healthy families
_____demonstrate commitment toward one another.
_____spend time together.
_____communicate effectively.
_____demonstrate appreciation for one another.
_____resolve conflicts in appropriate ways.
_____demonstrate commitment to their Christian faith.

How would you grade your family in each of these area? Use A for superior, B for above average, C for average, D for below average, and F for failure. If you feel comfortable doing so, explain the reason for the grade you gave your family.

Opening Prayer

Sing or speak together "Blest Be the Tie That Binds."

▼▼▼▼▼▼▼▼▼▼▼▼▼▼▼▼▼▼▼▼▼▼▼▼▼▼▼

1. Blest be the tie that binds
   Our hearts in Christian love;
   The unity of heart and mind
   Is like to that above.

2. Before our Father's throne
   We pour our ardent prayers;
   Our fears, our hopes, our aims are one,
   Our comforts and our cares.

3. We share our mutual woes,
   Our mutual burdens bear,
   And often for each other flows
   The sympathizing tear.

4. From sorrow, toil, and pain
   And sin we shall be free,
   And perfect love and friendship reign
   Through all eternity.

▲▲▲▲▲▲▲▲▲▲▲▲▲▲▲▲▲▲▲▲▲▲▲▲▲▲▲

Consider the Facts

Consider the following statistics. Then discuss the questions that follow.

• Almost 1 out of every 2.8 marriages end in divorce.

• Child abuse has risen 500% in the last 10 years.

• One in four girls under age 12 today will be sexually abused in her lifetime.

• Of the 3.6 million children who began schooling in 1986, 14% were children of unmarried parents, 40% will live in a broken home before they reach 18, and approximately 25% are latchkey children with no one to greet them when they come home from school.

- Every 30 minutes approximately 20 teens attempt suicide.
- Of the 33 million poor Americans, 13 million are children; 500,000 of those children are homeless.
- 39% of U.S. high school students don't graduate. The dropout rate for nonwhites is 40%.
- 56% of American families say they eat dinner together every day. The average time a family spends eating dinner is 32 minutes. 40% of all households eat dinner with the TV or VCR on.
- Fathers spend an average of 39 seconds a day in quality communication with their children.
- The average child watches four hours of television a day.
- By the time a child is 18 years old, he/she has witnessed 25,000 television murders.

1. Summarize
parent/child relationships described in the statistics.

a day in the life of an "average" family.

a day in the life of an "average" child.

2. What challenges do you see for parents in the future as you consider the statistics?

3. How does caring for aging parents affect your parenting?

4. How do the majority of Americans measure up to God's Word, "If anyone does not provide for his relatives, and especially for his immediate family, he has denied the faith and is worse than an unbeliever" (1 Timothy 5:8)?

5. How do you measure up to God's Word when you consider your parenting?

God's Word Speaks

We seek the wisdom that only God can provide us in His Word as we wrestle with the issues that surround parenting. What does God say about caring for our children and our attitude and responsibility to them? Read the following passages with pen in hand. Underline significant words and/or phrases.

Sons are a heritage from the LORD, children a reward from Him. (Psalm 127:3)

Train a child in the way he should go, and when he is old he will not turn from it. (Proverbs 22:6)

Love the LORD your God with all your heart and with all your soul and with all your strength. These commandments that I give you today are to be upon your hearts. Impress them on your children. Talk about them when you sit at home and when you walk along the road, when you lie down and when you get up. Tie them as symbols on your hands and bind them on your foreheads. Write them on the door-frames of your houses and on your gates. (Deuteronomy 6:5–9)

Fathers, do not exasperate your children; instead, bring them up in the training and instruction of the Lord. (Ephesians 6:4)

He who spares the rod hates his son, but he who loves him is careful to discipline him. (Proverbs 13:24)

People were bringing little children to Jesus to have Him touch them, but the disciples rebuked them. When Jesus saw this, He was indignant. He said to them, "Let the little children come to Me, and do not hinder them, for the kingdom of God belongs to such as these. (Mark 10:13–14)

We will not hide them from their children; we will tell the next generation the praiseworthy deeds of the LORD, His power, and the wonders He has done. He decreed statutes for Jacob and established the law in Israel, which He commanded our forefathers to teach their children, so the next generation would know them, even the children yet to be born, and they in turn would tell their children. (Psalm 78:4–6)

1. Summarize what God says about children in the verses found on the preceeding page.

2. How do you measure up to God's expectations for your attitude and responsibility toward your child(ren)? Put a mark on the line to describe how well you live up to God's expectations. Explain your answer.

|————————————————————————|
success   failure

3. If honest, most of us would have to admit that we don't *always* live up to God's high expectations. In fact, at times as we try to juggle meeting the needs of aging parents and growing children, we might consider ourselves failures. What does God's Word say to us as parents who at times fail miserably to live up to His expectations? Read the following verses from Psalm 103 with pen in hand. Underline those words and/or phrases that provide you comfort and hope in the midst of your failures and guilt.

▼▼▼▼▼▼▼▼▼▼▼▼▼▼▼▼▼▼▼▼▼▼▼▼▼

Praise the LORD, O my soul,
    and forget not all His benefits—
who forgives all your sins
    and heals all your diseases,
who redeems your life from the pit
    and crowns you with love and compassion,
who satisfies your desires with good things
    so that your youth is renewed like the eagle's.
The LORD works righteousness
    and justice for all the oppressed.
He made known His ways to Moses,
    His deeds to the people of Israel:
The LORD is compassionate and gracious,
    slow to anger, abounding in love.
He will not always accuse,
    nor will He harbor His anger forever;
He does not treat us as our sins deserve
    or repay us according to our iniquities.
For as high as the heavens are above the earth,
    so great is His love for those who fear Him;
as far as the east is from the west,
    so far has He removed our transgressions from us.
As a father has compassion on his children,
    so the LORD has compassion on those who fear
        Him;
for He knows how we are formed,
    He remembers that we are dust.
As for man, his days are like grass,
    he flourishes like a flower of the field;
the wind blows over it and it is gone,
    and its place remembers it no more.
But from everlasting to everlasting
    the LORD's love is with those who fear Him,
    and His righteousness with their children's children.
(Psalm 103:2–17)

▲▲▲▲▲▲▲▲▲▲▲▲▲▲▲▲▲▲▲▲▲▲▲▲▲

4. What assurance does God provide to parents who have at times failed to live up to God's expectations and to fulfill their God-given responsibilities?

5. God does not jump into a parent's life, forgive the parent for his or her sins, and exit to pursue more important details.

Read the following verses and summarize God's plan for you in Christ.

▼▼▼▼▼▼▼▼▼▼▼▼▼▼▼▼▼▼▼▼▼▼▼▼▼▼▼

The Word [Jesus] became flesh and made His dwelling among us [literally translated, "tented among us"]. (John 1:14)

I pray that out of His glorious riches He may strengthen you with power through His Spirit in your inner being, so that Christ may dwell in your hearts through faith. And I pray that you, being rooted and established in love, may have power, together with all the saints, to grasp how wide and long and high and deep is the love of Christ, and to know this love that surpasses knowledge—that you may be filled to the measure of all the fullness of God. (Ephesians 3:16–19)

Let the peace of Christ rule in your hearts, since as members of one body you were called to peace. And be thankful. Let the word of Christ dwell in you richly as you teach and admonish one another with all wisdom, and as you sing psalms, hymns and spiritual songs with gratitude in your hearts to God. (Colossians 3:15–16)

▲▲▲▲▲▲▲▲▲▲▲▲▲▲▲▲▲▲▲▲▲▲▲▲▲▲▲

6. What word or words recur in these verses?

7. How does Christ give you comfort and hope as you face the challenges of parenting and caring for aging parents?

Strengthening Your Family

Remember ... Healthy families
demonstrate commitment toward one another;
spend time together;
communicate effectively;
demonstrate appreciation for one another;
resolve conflicts in appropriate ways;
demonstrate commitment to their Christian faith.
Brainstorm some possible things you can do this week to build a healthier family as you focus on parenting.

Before the Next Session

1. Select one or two of the things you brainstormed to build a healthy family and put them into action this week. Plan to report on successes and/or challenges.

2. Reread the Scripture verses presented in this session. Write new insights the Holy Spirit provided you as you studied God's Word. Be prepared to share these insights at the beginning of the next session.

3. Pray that the Holy Spirit might strengthen the other families in the group as they seek to build healthier families through improved parenting.

Closing Prayer

Pray together that as the Word of Christ dwells in you richly, that the Holy Spirit might enable you to build a healthier family.

Soaring, Running, and Walking in the Sandwich Generation

Ice Breaker

What bird(s) best describes you in your relationship with parent(s) and child(ren) during the past week? Explain your choice.

_____ostrich

_____pelican

_____vulture

_____cuckoo bird

_____rooster

_____turkey

_____penguin

_____eagle

_____pigeon

_____chicken

_____love bird

_____other _____

Opening Prayer

Pray, reflecting on the following words from "On Eagle's Wings."

And God will raise you up on eagle's wings, bear you on the breath of dawn, make you to shine like the sun, and hold you in the palm of God's hand. [Amen.]

A Case Study from the Sandwich Generation

Read the following case study from the sandwich generation. Then discuss the questions.

Since my retirement I have enjoyed watching people in the park near my home. Yesterday, a van pulled up and out of it tumbled five active youngsters followed by a tired-looking woman in her mid-forties. I asked her, "Are all these kids yours or are you on your way to a picnic?"

"Yes, they're all mine," she answered, "and, believe me, its no picnic."

She then began to tell me about her life. This summer was especially difficult. She was only recently divorced from the husband who had abandoned her and the family. The children were now out of school for three months and occupying their time at home had become almost impossible. "If I'm not breaking up fights and cleaning up after them, I'm taking them to basketball camps, music camps, and dance camps or my mother to the doctor. Mom recently came to live with me. She is 86 and her health is deteriorating. Sometimes when the children get on her nerves, or she gets on their nerves, I bring the kids to the park."

I wanted to say something meaningful to this woman, but before I had a chance, she hurried off to tend to a child who had fallen off the swing and was crying. Then I remembered myself at this woman's stage of life. My mother-in-law lived with us, but she helped my wife with the children and brought a rich-ness to our family we would have otherwise not known. We too have five children, but my wife always seemed to enjoy devoting her summer days to them while I was at work. Times have sure changed, I reflected. Or have they?

1. What bird best describes the mother in the story? Explain.

_____ostrich

_____pelican

_____vulture

_____cuckoo bird

_____rooster

_____turkey

_____penguin

_____eagle

_____pigeon

_____chicken

_____love bird

_____other _____

2. What bird best describes the person telling the story? Explain.

_____ostrich

_____pelican

_____vulture

_____cuckoo bird

_____rooster

_____turkey

_____penguin

_____eagle

_____pigeon

_____chicken

_____love bird

_____other _____

39
▼

3. If you had the opportunity to speak to the mother, what would you say to her? Why?

4. If you had the opportunity to speak to the person telling the story, what would you say to him? Why?

5. Take some time now to share *your* story with a partner.

God's Word Speaks

Read aloud Isaiah 40:28–31.

▼▼▼▼▼▼▼▼▼▼▼▼▼▼▼▼▼▼▼▼▼▼▼▼▼▼▼▼

28 Do you not know?
    Have you not heard?
The LORD is the everlasting God,
    the Creator of the ends of the earth.
He will not grow tired or weary,
    and His understanding no one can fathom.
29 He gives strength to the weary
    and increases the power of the weak.

³⁰ Even youths grow tired and weary,
and young men stumble and fall;
³¹ but those who hope in the LORD
will renew their strength.
They will soar on wings like eagles;
they will run and not grow weary,
they will walk and not be faint. (Isaiah
40:28–31)

▲▲▲▲▲▲▲▲▲▲▲▲▲▲▲▲▲▲▲▲▲▲▲▲▲▲▲▲▲▲▲

1. These verses from Isaiah could be divided into three parts: 1—questions; 2—answers to the questions (vv. 28–29); 3—result and response to the answers (vv. 30–31). Summarize in your own words each of the three parts.

Questions **Answers to the Questions** **Result and Response**

2. Reread Isaiah 40:28–29. Describe the person to whom the answers are addressed. How or why might the answers be addressed to you or others living in the sandwich generation?

3. Circle the words "hope in the Lord." Then draw an arrow from these words to the results of faith. Next, draw additional arrows from the result of faith to the responses of those who are faithful.

4. As you reflect upon living in the sandwich generation, what words or phrases from Isaiah are particularly meaningful? Why?

5. But you may ask, "How might I strengthen and increase my 'hope in the Lord' so that as I experience the challenges of life in the sandwich generation I can be *renewed, soar, run,* and *walk?*" Let's examine God's Word for clues. With pen in hand underline words and/or phrases that are meaningful or helpful to you. Plan to share the words and/or phrases you underline.

▼▼▼▼▼▼▼▼▼▼▼▼▼▼▼▼▼▼▼▼▼▼▼▼▼

You have known the holy Scriptures, which are able to make you wise for salvation through faith in Christ Jesus. All Scripture is God-breathed and is useful for teaching, rebuking, correcting, and training in righteousness, so that the man of God may be thoroughly equipped for every good work. (2 Timothy 3:15–17)

For the Word of God is living and active. Sharper than any double-edged sword, it penetrates even to dividing soul and spirit, joints and marrow; it judges the thoughts and attitudes of the heart. (Hebrews 4:12–13)

Your word is a lamp to my feet and a light for my path. (Psalm 119:105)

As the rain and the snow come down from heaven, and do not return to it without watering the earth and making it bud and flourish, so that it yields seed for the sower and bread for the eater, so is My word that goes out from My mouth: It will not return to Me empty, but will accomplish what I desire and achieve the purpose for which I sent it. (Isaiah 55:10–11)

"As for God, His way is perfect; the word of the LORD is flawless. He is a shield for all who take refuge in Him." (2 Samuel 22:31)

▲▲▲▲▲▲▲▲▲▲▲▲▲▲▲▲▲▲▲▲▲▲▲▲▲▲▲

6. How does God continue to strengthen and increase our "hope [faith]" in Him?

7. How might your strengthened and increased faith enable you to share His love for you as you care for aging parents and children?

Life in the Sandwich Generation: A Soaring, Running, and Walking Experience

In Christ Jesus, God provides forgiveness for all sins and, in faith He empowers us to live lives of service that reflect His love for us. God continues to renew us and strengthen us as the Holy Spirit works through His Word. We cling to God's promises of strength and renewal as we find opportunities to study His Word.

Consider opportunities, new or existing, to continue your study of God's Word, so that He might renew and strengthen your life in the sandwich generation, enabling you to soar, run, and walk. Jot down your plans for continued involvement in Bible study and share them with your group. People in your group may be aware of additional opportunities. Or consider continuing to meet together as a small group to study God's Word.

Closing Prayer

Speak the words of Isaiah 40:28–31 responsively to one another:

 I: Do you not know?
 II: Have you not heard?
 I: The LORD is the everlasting God,
 II: The Creator of the ends of the earth.
 I: He will not grow tired or weary,
 II: and His understanding no one can fathom.
 I: He gives strength to the weary
 II: and increases the power of the weak.
 I: Even youths grow tired and weary,
 II: and young men stumble and fall;
 I: but those who hope in the LORD
 II: will renew their strength.
I and II: They will soar on wings like eagles;
  they will run and not grow weary,
  they will walk and not be faint.

▼▼▼▼▼▼▼▼▼▼▼▼▼▼▼▼▼▼▼▼▼▼▼▼▼▼

Leaders Notes

This study provides much opportunity for open-ended discussion. It will be important to keep the class moving and focused on the material. Encourage participants, especially those of the sandwich generation, to express their opinions and insights. Be sensitive for signals that your congregation needs an on-going ministry to the sandwich generation.

While the simple answer to all of our earthly struggles is to "trust in God," as Christians we are called upon to be the physical extension of Christ's body, the church. As God's Spirit works in the lives of His people, some may feel lead to "get involved" in ministry to sandwich generation families. If some members of the class display a keen interest in this subject or are willing to organize some of the suggested responses, make certain that the appropriate board or staff person is notified of this interest so that encouragement can be given to proceed.

▲▲▲▲▲▲▲▲▲▲▲▲▲▲▲▲▲▲▲▲▲▲▲▲▲

Session 1

The Big Squeeze

▲ Focus

Welcome everyone. Give each participant a copy of the Study Guide. Encourage participants to write their names on the front covers. Ask that they take the booklets home between sessions and bring them back each time the group meets.

▲ Objectives

By the power of the Holy Spirit working through God's Word participants will

1. define the term "sandwich generation" as it relates to heads of households who find themselves caring for their aging parents or grandparents and for their own children or grandchildren;

2. identify some of the challenges and opportunities experienced as members of the sandwich generation;

3. seek comfort and encouragement from God's promises that through Christ He provides rescue from sin, death, and the power of Satan and refuge "under His wings";

4. give thanks to God for sending Jesus to invite all who are weary and burdened to come to Him to receive rest.

▲ Ice Breaker

Have participants follow the instructions in the Study Guide. If time permits and your group is small enough, you may want to have each participant share his or her object with the entire group.

▲ Opening Prayer

Invite participants to pray with you the prayer printed in the Study Guide.

▲ Meet the Doe Family

Invite a volunteer to read the vignette aloud. Then have participants work independently to check the items that describe Jane Doe's feelings and/or thoughts. After participants have checked items describing Jane's feelings, direct them to draw a star next to the thoughts and feelings on the list that they have experienced. Have participants share their responses and a bit of their stories of life in the sandwich generation with a partner.

▲ Squeezed, but Not Squashed

Invite a volunteer to read aloud 1 Timothy 5:8. Have participants discuss the questions that follow either with a partner or with the entire group.

1. This verse may trouble Jane and the participants. If an individual is burdened with guilt for not providing adequately for relatives, this verse will be like "rubbing salt into a wound." Invite participants to share the thoughts and feelings that come to mind as they read this verse.

2. Accept all responses. Most participants will not check "wonderfully." Most caregivers feel that they could do more.

3. Although answers will vary, participants may have underlined "fowler's snare," "terror of night," "arrow that flies by day," "pestilence that stalks in the darkness," and "the plague that destroys at midday."

4. Again, answers will vary. Participants might have circled "You will not fear," "no harm will befall you," "no disaster will come near your tent," "I will rescue him," "I will protect him," "I will be with him in trouble," "I will deliver him in trouble," "I will deliver him," "With long life will I satisfy him," and "show him My salvation."

5. Emphasize that God provides us a rescue when we experience the big squeeze. Participants might have drawn a cross next to "I will rescue him," "I will deliver him," and "show him My salvation."

6. Provide time for participants to share with a partner.

7. Urge participants to read aloud Galatians 1:3–5 to a partner substituting the pronoun with the partner's name.

8. By Jesus' death on the cross and glorious victory from the dead on Easter morning, God has rescued us from our sins through His forgiveness, the present evil age, and death.

9. Answers will vary.

▲ Peace in the Midst of the Big Squeeze

Invite a volunteer to read aloud the opening paragraph. Then have participants work independently to underline Jesus' promises in Matthew 11:28–30. Then invite participants to write a prayer using the instructions in the Study Guide as guidelines.

▲ Before the Next Session

Urge participants to complete one or more of the suggested activities prior to the next session.

▲ Closing Worship

Invite volunteers to pray the prayers they wrote.

Session 2

Caring for Aging Parents

▲ Focus

Welcome everyone. Give newcomers a copy of the Study Guide. Encourage them to write their names on the front covers. Ask that they take the booklets home between sessions and bring them back each time the group meets.

▲ Objectives

By the power of the Holy Spirit working through God's Word participants will

1. identify our attitudes and those of others concerning the care of aging parents;

2. describe some of the challenges and opportunities of caring for aging parents;

3. summarize what God in His Word says about caring for the elderly;

4. praise God for the forgiveness He offers in Christ to those who have failed to honor their parents.

▲ Ice Breaker

Invite the participants to use the sentence starters as a springboard for discussion with a partner.

▲ Opening Prayer

Pray the prayer printed in the Study Guide.

▲ A Visit to the Doe Household

Invite a volunteer to read aloud the vignette. Discuss the questions that follow either with a partner or with the entire group. Answers will vary to both of the questions.

▲ The Sandwich Generation Speaks

Have each participant complete the survey independently. Then share the following statistical data that emerged from a recent Gallup Poll that asked these questions.

1. 37% have not yet brought up the topic with them; 36% have talked generally but made no plans; 12% have discussed plans for finances, housing, and medical care but have no legal documentation for their plans; 14% have actually worked together to draw up legal documents for finances, housing, and medical care; 1% don't know.

2. 28%, they'll suffer disabilities that will force them to live in a nursing home; 26%, they'll die suddenly without the chance to say good-bye; 19%, they'll end up in a hospital being kept alive by machines; 14%, their need for ongoing medical care will force them to sell their home or spend their life's savings; 13%, don't know.

3. 85%, yes; 6%, no; 9%, don't know.

4. 66%, yes; 20%, no; 14%, don't know.

5. 84%, favor; 13%, oppose; 3%, don't know.

6. 56%, yes; 38%, no; 6%, don't know.

7. 52%, yes; 39%, no; 9%, don't know.

8. 85%, yes; 12%, no; 3%, don't know.

9. 77%, would insist doctors abide by their parent's instructions under all circumstances; 13%, overrule those instructions and authorize treatment if doctors recommend it; 10% don't know.

Take time for participants to answer the questions that follow the survey. Answers will vary to the questions.

▲ God's Word Speaks

Read aloud the opening paragraphs. Direct participants to underline significant words and/or phrases that indicate what God desires for our attitude and responsibility to be toward the elderly.

1. God says we should respect the elderly, honor them, and obey them.

2. At times we all fail to measure up to God's expectations for us. Answers will vary. Direct participants to put a mark on the continuum to describe how well they see themselves living up to God's expectations. Invite volunteers to share where they put their marks on the continuum.

3. Read aloud in unison the words of David in Psalm 32:1–5, 8–11.

Have participants refer to Psalm 32 to help them answers questions 4–6.

4. God offers forgiveness through faith in Christ Jesus to all who have failed to live up to His high standards.

5. Answers will vary. Invite volunteers to share their responses. Do not force anyone to share.

6. Answers will vary. Hopefully, participants will suggest additional opportunities they may have to study God's Word. You may want to encourage group members to read God's Word privately, involve themselves in family and individual devotions, and attend worship.

7. Urge participants to write a prayer using the guidelines found in the Study Guide. Have participants save the prayers they write to share as the closing for the session.

▲ Before the Next Session

Urge participants to complete one or more of the suggested activities prior to the next session.

▲ Closing Prayer

Invite volunteers to pray the prayers they wrote earlier as the closing.

Session 3

Bringing Up Children

▲ Focus

Welcome everyone. Give each newcomer a copy of the Study Guide. Encourage all participants to write their names of the front covers. Ask that they take the booklets home between sessions and bring them back each time the group meets.

▲ Objectives

By the power of the Holy Spirit working through God's Word participants will

1. draw conclusions from recent statistics about growing up in the nineties;

2. describe some of the challenges and opportunities of raising children in the nineties;

3. summarize what God says in His Word about caring for children;

4. express trust in God for the forgiveness He provides for our parenting failures and for His promise to strengthen, encourage, and guide us as we care for our children.

▲ Ice Breaker

Invite participants to share their answers to one of questions with a partner. Urge all participants to grade their families in the six areas listed. If participants feel comfortable doing so, invite them to share their responses with a partner.

▲ Opening Prayer

Sing or speak together the stanzas from "Blest Be the Tie That Binds."

▲ Consider the Facts

Invite volunteers to read aloud the statistics.

1. Answers will vary. Participants will probably indicate that relationships are strained and families are struggling. Don't spend too much time on these sentence starters.

2. Answers will vary.

3. Although answers will vary, participants will probably indicate that caring for aging parents strains their parenting abilities.

4. The statistics indicate that the majority of Americans have a difficult time measuring up to God's expectations for families. Remind participants that God shares His expectations for us in Matthew 5:48, "Be perfect."

5. Answers will vary. Most parents will admit that they have often failed as parents.

▲ God's Word Speaks

Invite volunteers to read aloud the Scripture passages. Suggest that other participants underline words and/or phrases that are most significant to them. Have participants complete independently questions one and two that follow the Scripture passages.

1. God says that children are *a reward*, that we should *train them*, that we should *discipline them*, that we should *not exasperate them*, and that we should *teach them God's Word*.

2. Invite volunteers to share where they put the mark on the continuum and why they put the mark at that place. Don't force anyone to share.

3. Read aloud this paragraph. Emphasize that God provides comfort and hope for parents who at times fail to live up to His expectations. Invite a volunteer or volunteers to read aloud the selected verses from Psalm 103. Urge participants to underline the words and/or phrases that provide them comfort and hope in the midst of failure and guilt. After reading aloud the verse ask volunteers to share the words and/or phrases they underlined.

4. The psalm assures us that God will not harbor His anger toward us forever, will forgive us, has compassion on us, is compassionate and gracious towards us, and His love for us is everlasting. God in Christ forgives us of all of our

sins. By His love we are motivated to serve Him as parents.

5. Through faith, Christ dwells in us. He remains with us at all times and in all places.

6. *Dwell* recurs in these verses.

7. If God is for us, who can be against us? As He dwells in us through faith, Christ provides us complete forgiveness for all of our sins and empowers and enables us to face the challenges of parenting and caring for aging parents.

▲ Strengthening Your Family

Read aloud the list. Then invite participants to work in small groups to create a list of ways to build healthier families as they are empowered by the love of Christ. Share lists with the entire group.

▲ Closing Prayer

Pray together that, as the Word of Christ dwells in you richly, you will build healthier families.

▲ Before the Next Session

Urge participants to complete one or more of the suggested activities prior to the next session.

Session 4

Soaring, Running, and Walking in the Sandwich Generation

▲ Focus

Welcome everyone to this final session. Make sure everyone has a copy of the Study Guide. Briefly review the preceeding three sessions.

▲ Objectives

By the power of the Holy Spirit working through God's Word participants will

1. identify some of the challenges of those living as the sandwich generation;

2. share some of the challenges they face as they care for their children and aging parents;

3. affirm the promises of God found in His Word—"gives strength to the weary, increases the power of the weak, will renew their strength, and they will soar on wings of eagles";

4. develop a plan to seek the Lord's comfort and guidance provided in His Word;

5. recognize caring for an aging parent(s) and child(ren) as opportunities God provides for us to share the love God in Christ has shown to us.

▲ Ice Breaker

Read the directions aloud. Have fun with the activity.

▲ Opening Prayer

Lead the group in prayer, reflecting on the words from "On Eagle's Wings."

▲ A Case Study from the Sandwich Generation

Invite a volunteer to read aloud the case study. Discuss the questions that follow with a partner or in small groups. Answers will vary. Invite volunteers to share their stories of living in the sandwich generation with a partner or in small groups.

▲ God's Word Speaks

Invite a volunteer(s) to read aloud Isaiah 40:28–31. Have participants complete the chart.

1. Column 1 would include the questions, "Do you not know?" and "Have you not heard?" Column 2 would include "the Lord is God," "He will not grow tired," and "He gives strength to the weary." Column 3 would include "the Lord will renew their strength," "they will soar on wings like eagles," "they will run and not grow weary," and "they will walk and not be faint."

2. It seems that these words were written for someone who was weary from the burdens in life. Life in the sandwich generation is often burdened. Remind participants that God invites those who are burdened to come to Him.

3. Direct participants to circle the words "hope in the Lord." Then direct participants to draw arrows using the directions in the Study Guide.

4. Answers will vary.

5. Invite participants to share the words they underlined.

6. The Holy Spirit works through God's Word to strengthen and increase our faith.

7. Through faith strengthened by the power of the Holy Spirit working through God's Word we are motivated, equipped, and empowered to share Jesus' love with others.

▲ Life in the Sandwich Generation: A Soaring, Running, and Walking Experience

Read aloud and then discuss ways in which the members of the group could find additional opportunities to study God's Word so that their faith might be renewed and strengthened.

▲ Closing Prayer

Speak responsively to one another Isaiah 40:28–31 as a closing prayer.